Also By Tevin Curtis Ryan Dubé

Book Of The Enlightened One

Amen: A Great Light Within Divine Darkness

The Mystery Behind Life, Death and Resurrection

A Silent Truth

SELF

PSALMS FROM A NEW KING DAVID

Tevin C. R. Dubé

© 2019 Tevin Curtis Ryan Dubé. All rights reserved.

ISBN: 978-976-96334-0-7

Publishers Note

No part of this publication may be reproduced, stored in, or introduced into a retrieval system, or transmitted in any form or by means (electronic, mechanical, photocopying, recording, or otherwise) without prior consent of the copyright owner.

Tevin Curtis Ryan Dubé

Trinidad and Tobago

Email: tevindube@yahoo.com

Facebook Page –Tevin 'Mystical' Dube

Instagram – mystical_dube

Twitter – @mysticaldube

Cover Design by Tevin C. R. Dubé

Contents

Introduction............................7

Foreword..................................9

Psalm 1 – 7......................................11-23

Psalm 8 – 14....................................24-39

Psalm 15 – 21..................................40-57

Psalm 22 – 28..................................58-73

Psalm 29 – 35..................................74-88

Psalm 36 – 42..................................89-104

Psalm 43 – 49..................................105-119

Psalm 50 – 52..................................120-123

Introduction

The most popular book compilation throughout the entire Bible in my estimation is that of The Book of Psalms. It is the most historically accurate piece of truth to ever be told within. To answer your curiosity, it's because out of the other books, it deals with the occurrences of Life on a day-to-day basis.

Psalms are a standout factor because they speak directly to SELF about SELF for the help of SELF from SELF ITSELF. It did indeed pave the way for The Proverbs.

Psalms in their truest form are a direct communication between the Lower Self and Higher Self to become centered and well-balanced by a Mastered Self. It is the Holy Communion between the Ultimate Source Divine and the Man of Spirit.

It is to be perfectly aligned with the Universal Most High Supreme Divine Being that is infinitely beyond antiquity eternally.

Foreword

These words that you are about to read will have a very direct impact on you in the best way possible. Intuitively, I heard to write my personal Psalms because they would be a very present help in times of need.

"My heart is inditing a good matter: I speak of the things which I have made touching the king: my tongue is the pen of a ready writer." – Psalm 45:1 KJV

The only Psalm I have ever committed to memory is Psalm 23 which is still my all-time favourite. Even the rendition of it sung by reggae icons Buju Banton and Gramps Morgan added soul to give it even more Life rhythmically.

This book in particular has naturally been aligned numerologically. Number 7 is the most spiritual number that is aligned with teaching. Whoever has this number in their natal chart placements can be naturally inclined as an intellectualiser, writer and musician—apart from those in possession of the highest number; the number 9. I have both in the right places hence I am made to conduct such works naturally. This will be my 7th official book to be published which contains a sum of 52 personal Psalms that yet still equates to the number 7 (5+2). The total amount of pages of this book ends at 124 (1+2+4=7); surprised indeed yet still not surprising.

The divine inspiration inherited is what is channelled into those divine words of mystical proportions. The same forces that grant such a profound overstanding unto such a one shall be the same that will help you to gain such fullness and beyond that which isn't even stated.

Therefore, as you read, relate with every word, own these Psalms and make them yours and establish a mutual but unbreakable connection between you and the Holy Most High Supreme Divine that can still be found within YOU.

The time has come for you to discover that which is unlimited within you. It is time to unlock your fullest potential and truth to unlock your divine purpose and finally take full control of your destiny that was solely intended for you.

Dedicate To All Those In Need

PSALM 1

O blessed Divine in thy Holy Tabernacle;

2 Thou have heard my prayers.

3 I acknowledged my imbalances and shortcomings unto Thee and Thou have rectified my imbalances.

4 When my mind was greatly troubled and my heart was heavy, sinking deep within my soul;

5 Thou have returned, flying mightily to my aid and my rescue.

6 Thou have thoroughly purged me, making sure that even my bones were sparkling.

7 My head glowed with a great light to that of the sun.

8 Shame has Thou wiped from my eyes and hid before the faces of men.

9 Mercy is the seat which You sit upon O Holy Divine.

10 Many years shall I be in peace because of thy everlasting glory. Amen and Amen.

PSALM 2

Praises be unto the Universal Supreme Being, the Most Majestic, the One that is filled with Holy Cosmic Anointing.

2 O Holy Power which begat the Holy Trinity itself;

3 Unto Thee I do lay my supplications.

4 I ask of Thee to sift out my enemies as wheat.

5 As they lay wait for my soul, You lay wait beneath them as well.

6 Thou have revealed the enemies to me, even within my dreams as I lay to rest.

7 The Most High Divine is beyond the powers of being omnipotent.

8 There is no limit to Your limitless nature.

9 I felt the steps of death compassing and my soul was greatly troubled.

10 I cried within my troubled soul and invoked the very Source of the Most Mighty Divine.

11 Thou dropped pillars of lightening upon the heads of those that prosecuted me.

12 The Supreme Divine of Hosts burned all witchcraft and the hands that were behind such.

13 Though no man is perfect, the Most High Divine of Hosts destroyed many that are against those who suffer daily because of their iniquities and has beseeched Thy precious Presence in forgiveness.

14 The Most High Divine cleanses, the Most High Supreme purges, the Great Divine redeems and Thou art the Most Holy over all things.

15 Those that walk in their own way but against the Supreme One shall be utterly plucked out.

16 Their destruction will come suddenly and at times unaware.

17 When they worry, they shall suffer greatly.

18 But as soon as they celebrate, their peril shall swoop in and they are no more.

19 As for me I will continue to diligently practice my trust in the Universal Divine and give thanks.

20 My soul shall truly be happy when the bitterest of my enemies are shut up within their graves.

PSALM 3

The burdens of my transgressions have become too much for me to bear.

2 A heavy conscience is the greatest of all loads to carry.

3 My very life has become an obstacle to my body.

4 The more I live the more I suffer from the mistakes of my youth.

5 Forgive me O Great Divine of Hosts. Free the burdens of my guilt.

6 When my eyes couldn't see beyond my transgressions, I felt my soul cut off from existing.

7 Rise said the Most High intuitively, get up from your pit of sorrow and know that your imbalances are pardoned.

8 There is nothing too hard for me; the same One who created all creations from a simple thought.

9 I know the heart and reins of all living things.

10 Shall I not compass thee about and deliver thee thoroughly?

11 Thou saw it fit to give me thyself as a living sacrifice.

12 I saw the brokenness of thy

heart; thy spirit was truly contrite and I have accepted your sacrifice willingly.

13 At once, I heard thy prayers and I sent my Seraphims and Cherubs to protect you at all times.

14 Thou have heightened my life before my oppressors.

15 My eyes shall behold their demise and I shall be their end.

16 Thou has pardoned all my iniquities and released the burdens of my imbalances.

17 The Great Divine, even my Higher Self quieted the guilty pangs of my conscience that I may lift Thy Holy Name on high.

PSALM 4

Put new prayers in mouth O Most Holy Divine.

2 Protect me with all the waters of the world that are roundabout and even deep within.

3 Protect me as with the depths of the oceans which the flesh of men is yet unable to explore.

4 Protect me from my enemies by hiding me as a grain of sugar upon the shores of the seas.

5 Hide me as a grain of salt amidst sifted flour.

6 Protect me within the core of the Earth and hide me within the hidden cleft of the rock.

7 Let me disappear before my foes as a shadow within the shades of darkness.

8 Blessed be the name of the Most High Supreme Divine Being who dwells from everlasting unto everlasting. Selah.

9 Expose my enemies as a shadow when bright light is cast upon things in the dark.

10 Make immune, my flesh from fire and hide me amidst the molten lava.

11 Burn them up with thy anger which is seven times hotter than the worst volcanic eruption.

PSALM 5

The enemy dug a deep pit. Oh, how deep a pit!

2 Indeed a plentiful rain did fall and delayed my steps.

3 The Supreme One had prevented me in times of trouble that I may sit still and rest at the right hand of the Most High Divine.

4 Thou prepared my meals and indeed it was good; I was strengthened to move forward.

5 As I swam over the depths which the enemy had made, their faces became crooked at the anointed one.

6 They rejoiced as they saw the strength of his hands and feet begin to fail.

7 Lo and behold the Most High Divine came as a light wood adrift.

8 The faces of my foes twisted further at the man who tried to be good.

9 The Universal Supreme was before them and blind they were.

10 Their own pit had prevented them from passing over unto glory.

11 Let the pure in heart rejoice and the

clean in mind sing praises.

12 The Sweet One that sits on high but yet still roams the low shall save all those that acknowledge Thee.

PSALM 6

Thou have descended from the heavens and sat firmly upon my head as a crown most precious.

2 My head now shines with glory as thy Presence can be found within and with me.

3 Thou have seen my head fit to rest upon and ordained it to be holy as Thy Mercy Seat.

4 The blessings of Thy Majesty are better than Life itself.

5 Thou rested upon me as light as a feather in which I rejoiced day and night.

6 But when Thou descended upon they who were against me, they screamed before the weight of Thee.

7 Sore troubles and vexation of spirit became their portion.

8 Their lamentations drowned in the great abyss.

9 They mock the Most High Supreme with evil for good;

10 They walked and talked sanctimoniously over their kin and forget that all men err.

11 Their own ways had now encompassed them and they were caught.

12 My Omniversal Divine, the Essence of

my Being, kept me
steadfast all day and
night long.

PSALM 7

Let my words be forged from in Your midst O blessed Divine and be new prayers of acceptance unto Thee.

2 I beseech Thee to bless me with truthful knowledge, wisdom and overstanding.

3 Bless me with knowledge, wisdom and overstanding as the dust of the Earth.

4 Bless me with this Holy Trinity as the drops of the seas combined.

5 Bless me with this Holy Key to Existence as the drops from the heavy rainfall.

6 Grant it unto me as the trees within the forests and even the leaves that are thereupon.

7 Bestow it upon me as the grasses of the Earth.

8 Open up my being unto the knowledge of the Universe more than the stars within each galaxy.

9 I humbly request of Thee to be my personal tutor in that I shall never go wrong.

10 Thou have quickened my mind unto the possibilities of being limitless.

11 Therefore, excellent is the name of the Absolute Supreme Being of

infinite supra-consciousness and beyond perpetually.

PSALM 8

O Merciful Supreme, the Highest Divine;

2 Thou Art the Holiest One of all things.

3 Thou Art the Formless One that gave all forms.

4 Thou Art the Shapeless One that forms all shapes of perpetuating geometry infinitely.

5 Thou Art the Great Presence.

6 How mighty Art Thou O Holy Divine?

7 What is the measure of Thy strength?

8 The great Divine is Most Supreme and is beyond omnipotence.

9 Unto Thee do I put my trust and in Thee do I have a confident expectancy.

10 Thou Art magnificent in that Thou are pure in nature and are the main Source amidst the essence of all energies.

11 Thou Art the Force that made Life itself to be alive.

12 Thou Art the Existence which makes all existences possible.

13 The elevation of thoughts towards Thee is in no wise worthy to explain Thy ineffable nature. Yet

still I am privileged to house such within me.

14 I will continue to devote myself to Thee O Most Mighty Divine through the alignment of both my lower and higher self.

15 Thy tender mercies and loving kindnesses existed before aeons in that it is wise for me to trust Thee all the day long.

16 Because of the Most High Supreme, my life is made to be of complete fullness.

PSALM 9

The proof of Thee lies in the mystical nature of all things.

2 Truly a fool says in their heart that the Holy Divine Supreme One is nonexistent.

3 Such a one is so weak in spirit that their husk feels invincible because they are unable to balance their ego.

4 In no wise can the flesh truly be compared to the Spirit of the Most High Divine because the flesh is only in possession of a minuscule spark.

5 The foolish man blasphemed against the Universe and is yet still unaware from whence he truly came.

6 Ego makes him feel superior in fickle flesh yet still he has no power over gravity.

7 He cannot stop the rays from the sun from emitting;

8 In which he could never stop the natural process of precipitation.

9 He still cannot ward off the strength of sleep or number the hairs on his head.

10 The fool still cannot comprehend that all human life is subjected to the principles of the flesh.

11 The Divine One is real and coming to know SELF will make it to become axiomatic.

12 As for me, my humility is extended because of Thee.

13 O Great Divine; O merciful internal Saviour Divine, free up the burden of my human iniquities and imbalances that I may dwell in peace.

PSALM 10

Be humble and bless the Great Divine even the Most High.

2 A tree may soar towards the heavens but its height would be in vain if it's not properly grounded.

3 The beauty of a tall building would not be possible without the hidden foundation it is erected.

4 An eagle may fly all day yet it still needs to come down at night time.

5 Be humble and bless the Great Divine with gratitude.

6 A lake is not made possible without higher banks.

7 One may be a great swimmer but you still need the shallow waters near the shores.

8 You may be high but for a moment as one can be easily abased.

9 You may be low and all of a sudden one can be easily exalted.

10 In all that ye do, one must remember to always give thanks. Never be without heartfelt gratitude at all times possible.

11 Be humble and bless the Great Divine even the innermost Saviour Divine.

PSALM 11

O merciful Most High Divine quiet down the pangs of my mind.

2 What may seem inevitable unto me is not at all inevitable unto Thee.

3 It would have appeared unto King David that his fate was inevitable when his enemies encamped against the sweet psalmist.

4 Thou had lifted his voice unto the Most High Divine and behold the Saviour Divine diverted storms.

5 O Holy One of my soul, the end of my flesh comes as a result of death.

6 In the end, this is the result of both the divine and the heathen walking around in flesh form.

7 The days of the flesh are a daily sacrifice.

8 Be merciful unto me that I may not perish before my time.

9 Satisfy my belly with the sustenance of Thy Divine joy and make strong my bones.

10 Protect me because of thy tender mercies sake and let the hairs of my head turn grey.

11 Thou shall never be slack concerning Thy promise to always be

with me and to guide me through.

12 The most High of King David shall also be my help. The same Saviour Divine I beseech and call upon because Thou Art Most Mighty.

13 Be for me as Thou had been faithful unto the King.

14 Be delighted in my sight, for my heart greatly moved the Great Divine that Thou have gained eternal favour for me unlike another.

15 My soul shall not perish by the hands of the wicked because the Most High Divine had anointed me forever. Selah.

PSALM 12

In my times of low, I have known the Most Mighty Divine.

2 In my times of low I have come to find myself.

3 When my thoughts had forsaken me, my strength came from a Source that was beyond my soul.

4 Blessed be the natural mystic of the Most Mystical Divine.

5 Thou had revealed great a secret unto me;

6 My humility shall always remind me that I am a mere man of the flesh even though I'm in possession of an immortal spirit.

7 Hence, my past transgressions and mistakes were not intended to place me into the solitude of death.

8 When the people of Israel ate unleavened bread and bitter grapes at Passover;

9 It was to remind them of the bitter days of bondage with the intent for them to be grateful for the sweetness of their deliverance.

10 Through the Earth's faults it is perfected.

11 I shall ever so often reflect upon my own transgression against

Thee O Most Supreme Divine on high.

12 My thoughts shall no longer be burdened through overthinking and the guiltiness of my iniquities.

13 Such is the revelation revealed unto this unworthy yet still worthy vessel.

14 My reflection shall ever so often remind me to keep in Thy Presence O Holy Divine.

15 Through my repeated mistakes I have been perfected before Thy Holy Face.

16 Because of it I shall never lose my footing.

17 The foundation of my salvation I shall never forget.

18 The eagle soaring all day must rest low at night but yet still perched atop the highest tree.

19 O my Divine, you make me to soar high but as I rest, my abode is yet still high up in Thy Holy Mountain.

20 My feet shall be deep as strong roots of a tree planted by the living waters of Life.

21 But my meditation shall be high as the continuous heavens because the redemption of the Innermost Divine is dwelling within me.

PSALM 13

Once I was young and low in spirit;

2 My self-esteem was indeed far from me.

3 Not knowing the worth of my life, I was bought by the cheap pleasures of being imbalanced that yet still cost me greatly.

4 I called upon Thee O Great One when I was still tender of age.

5 I prayed unto Thee many nights with teary eyes because of the cleanliness of my heart.

6 Even though my hands became marred from the blackness of being imbalanced, my mind was yet still pure.

7 I said unto my Supreme Being to forgive the weakness of my flesh and strengthen me from repeating my own hurt and sore regrets.

8 I am sinful and not worthy to be used by You and yet still, I found myself to be doing great things.

9 O Universal Supreme, will Thou use me to be great as Moses or as Noah? This I prayed as a youth.

10 Saviour Divine, I'm sure that Thou would not look upon someone like me.

11 There are far much better people for you to attend unto than to look upon someone like me.

12 O Most High, there are many who believe in you more than me so You probably don't even hear my prayers.

13 Forgive my sins and have mercy upon me Saviour Divine.

14 Surely out of the billions of people alive today, what would make me think that You would choose me from everyone else to do something so great as Noah and Moses?

15 O Divine, this I asked of You: Deal with everyone else and leave me for last.

16 Deal with the world first so when I call, You shall deal with me alone.

17 Surely the Supreme Divine accepted my prayers of offering when my soul was broken and my heart was filled with contrite.

18 The Most High Divine had looked upon my infirmities and had greatly blessed me.

19 Thou had truly set Thy sight upon the child that was low in thoughts but high in spirit.

20 Thou had exceedingly blessed me with greatness.

21 Thou had already spiritually anointed and appointed me.

22 Truly the Most High Divine Supreme Being had chosen me.

PSALM 14

Marvellous is the sound of Thy Voice that echoes loudly within me intuitively.

2 I heard at first and many times I disobeyed.

3 Some consider it as one's instincts but today I know it is much more.

4 Yeah, it is my personal guidance.

5 It is the Holy One calling out from the wilderness within my soul.

6 Yea, Thy Voice is an oasis springing out from the desert within my soul.

7 Thy deep voice speaks to me loudly from the depths of silence given by a still tongue and an overly observant foresight.

8 Thy Voice gave me sight when I was blinded for many years.

9 Thy Voice gave me sight beyond sight.

10 Thy Voice heightened all my senses and made me become superhuman.

11 Because of Thy Divine Voice, I gained the balanced sight of Universal Perception.

12 I no longer see things from the mundane.

13 My speech has changed greatly because of the perfection of the words of Thy Divine Voice.

14 Yea, though my flesh is of the carnal; my mind has been woven with the Divine Source.

15 Surely Thou shall guide me always.

16 Surely this body is a great temple.

17 It is the Holy Tabernacle of the Most High Divine.

18 Thy Divine Voice is greatly heard and is recognisable to me as plain as the stars in the heavens at night.

19 Thou Art truly within me and I never would have known such if I had never decided to know myself initially.

20 All along, the Great Divine was abiding within the depths of my unbounded soul patiently awaiting my-self discovery. Amen and Amen.

PSALM 15

The Most High Divine I call upon Thee.

2 O Supreme Divinity of the highest I do regard Thee, Selah.

3 Words are merely an expression of voice.

4 The consideration of my thoughts is high but yet still low when it is regarding the true nature of the Most Holy One.

5 Thou Art the great I AM; both the Divine Masculine and Divine Feminine energies combined. Selah.

6 I AM THAT I AM; Thou Art the great All in All.

7 The Lord of Hosts is a fraction of Thy true name professed by the great King David that was established by his hands.

8 Truly the Great One has many abodes.

9 In a stone surely, Thou can be found with the All-Seeing Eye.

10 Yea, I say this with great assurance because Thou have opened up my Eye to see.

11 Yea, when the "I" is made single, then the body becomes filled with the purity of liquid light.

12 In the presence of death, Thou are alive and well.

13 Thou have proven such unto me as with a seed that is planted.

14 Surely the seed dies at first but the eye within is filled with eternal Life.

15 Thou Art the Most Holy of Holies; Thou Art the Supreme Being of cosmic proportions and beyond comprehension.

16 Thou Art the everlasting vastness of the heavens and are yet still that which is beyond the Great Beyond of infinity infinitely.

17 Thou Art higher than the order of gender manifestation in pure form but take on such within us.

18 Thou Art all things combined and is still beyond all things combined. Even though a part of all things Thou can yet still be apart from it all independently.

19 My heart knows not thy true name because Thou Art chose to remain nameless just to be named by those of the spirit. Thy identity is truly a divine secret to be eternally discovered.

20 Thy Origins was already in existence long before existence even existed.

21 Therefore, I call Thee the Great Divine; the Most High

Supreme Divine Being; the Absolute One.

22 Thou know not a boundary for the bounds of the Great Divine is way beyond that of infinity.

23 Thou Art the pureness of all forces and energies. The manifestation of Thyself can still be found within the mortal realm of flesh.

PSALM 16

O Holy Divine in Thy Presence is bliss forevermore.

2 Thou have never changed Thyself because Thou Art the essence of a change that is yet still unchangeable.

3 Thy face has never changed from being amidst the centre of a peace that is so divine.

4 For this, Thy tender mercies and loving kindnesses have been ever of old.

5 The meekness of the Most Divine has always remained fixated.

6 It is when we choose to venture away from Thy Holy Presence Your appearance changes; even when we choose to be disconnected from ourselves.

7 It is so because of the many different positions we tend to place ourselves in.

8 A full-grown elephant can look as small as an ant in the distance.

9 From up high, a great cistern, even a great reservoir can look as small as a glass of water.

10 My soul shall remain at ease because I know my Great and Most Holy

Divine shall always be the same from time to eternity.

11 Blessings be upon the Most High Supreme Divine Being for divinely blessing my life with a perpetual cosmic endowment.

PSALM 17

The Great Blessed Divine, Thou Art the Great Examiner of the inner mind and heart.

2 Words can be expressed as a result of the tongue; they can be used to help explain a greater phenomenon.

3 Words are equipped to bring to the forefront one's thoughts.

4 Thou knows that no one that is in flesh, seldom be without fault.

5 None is perfect, yea I say; none is perfect in all that they think, say and do.

6 O, how much have I suffered from those that hate me?

7 They plot against my life by any means.

8 In secret they hide themselves to practice works of witchcraft, wizardry and sorcery to launch psychic attacks.

9 How much have I suffered because of my imperfections in accepting dangerous blows?

10 Yea, I will no longer accept the punishment that not even the Most Divine had wished upon me.

11 The Most High had pardoned me long before my transgressions but yet

still do I suffer my soul to death.

12 Be still and forgive thyself ye children of the Most Divine.

13 No longer shall ye tremble in fear of the enemy.

14 Thou shall not be ashamed and be made a reproved amongst the children of men.

15 The wicked shall now naturally fear you for the fear they brought upon you. It would be the works of their conscience.

16 Walk upright and straight in face but be patient and humble in mind and heart.

17 Watch as your enemies tremble and perish before your own eyes.

18 The Great Divine said unto my Lord, this is the power I have given unto thee.

19 The most venomous snake shall fear your toxicity.

20 The bones of your foes are white and dried up within their flesh. Their marrow is long gone.

21 The grave called unto them and yea in fear do they embrace it.

22 The coldness of their pits they greet warmly and suddenly because the Great Divine is far from their faces.

23 The Great Examiner has searched out their reins and they acknowledge not the Grand Supreme in all their ways.

24 They hide their transgressions from Thee and have become a bomb of corruption just waiting to explode upon the innocent ones trying.

25 Surely, they are no more, therefore; my heart shall greatly rejoice because I can walk freely.

26 My soul shall truly be at ease when those who intentionally and maliciously fight against me are sealed deep within their sepulchres. For they strive against my soul without a cause.

27 They have never forgiven to be forgiven. Yea, none is perfect and I acknowledge my errors daily and never wish harm upon anyone. Therefore, the Great Divine shall avenge me every time I call upon Thee for assistance. Amen.

PSALM 18

When the sun is sweltering, the flesh cries out for the rain.

2 When the rain is falling rampantly, the flesh cries out for the sun.

3 O thou mortal man, what could ever please thy perpetually hollow shell.

4 You can't pray for the rain and then become angry with the mud.

5 You can't pray for the sun and then become angry with the drought.

6 Be balanced in all your ways and lift thy eyes upon the Holy Pillars of Stability.

7 When there is dry weather, the time is right to prepare a proper walkway;

8 Therefore, the mud could never affect thee in any wise.

9 When the weather is dry, the time is right to prepare proper cisterns.

10 Therefore, when the rain pours heavily from the heavens, thou shall preserve much water.

11 In drought ye shall yet still drink bountifully.

12 In great floods shall your bridge be profoundly exalted.

13 Open up thy eyes unto the perfect balance of the power of the Holy Trinity, even Haile Selassie I.

14 The Great Divine is both the clean path through thick mud and the great reservoir in drought.

15 Because of Thy Holy knowledge, wisdom and complete overstanding my journey has become the fulfilment of my purpose.

16 Every season in your life is to prepare you for the next.

17 I shall be great because I am made to be great because of the greatness of the Most High Divine. Selah.

PSALM 19

O merciful Divine,

2 Let my heart be filled with joy and let my soul be in perfect merriment.

3 The enemy of my thoughts shall no longer steal my joy.

4 My bones were greatly weakened, yea many became feeble indeed.

5 The enemy that is within is greater than any physical foe that is without.

6 O Saviour Divine, the greatest burden is my own conscience.

7 A man may run unto the ends of the Earth but he surely cannot escape himself.

8 O Great Divine, let Thy Glorious Light shine upon my soul.

9 Grant me that peace which is imperative unto the longevity of my soul.

10 Amidst war shall I yet still be in peace.

11 Amidst sorrow but yet still shall I be in joy because of Thee.

12 The rod of correction shall be removed from me because of the obedience of my heart.

13 The Supreme Divine is the very Containment for the human conscience

that can get out of hand and control when left on our own.

14 Thou shall quiet the mind from overthinking and pessimism.

15 O Merciful Saviour Divine,

16 Let my heart be filled with joy and let my soul be in perfect peace. Amen. Selah.

PSALM 20

I was made to shine as the very night itself.

2 Only to the carnal eyes the light of the night appears to be darkness.

3 But O, how dark is truly the night?

4 I am comely, my skin glistens as the midnight continuum.

5 My hair is thick and stretches upwards to the heavens.

6 A masterpiece crafted by the powers of the Most High Divine I am indeed.

7 The darkness of the day is in no comparison to the light that is upon me.

8 To the carnal eyes, the darkness of the day is seen as a bright light.

9 The heavens are always bright because the light of the night existed before all beginnings.

10 The stars are made visible because of this Divine Light.

11 But the darkness of the day is truly blinding unto such a sight.

12 Blessed be the Absolute Divine Most High Divine.

13 Truly, were I wonderfully and beautifully made in

the very essence of the Most Holy Divine One.

14 The Most Holy Divine, Thou Art this everlasting and perpetual Light that existed before all things. Asé.

PSALM 21

Yea, surely I have entreated good things for my enemies.

2 I prayed deeply for their salvation.

3 I dealt with them in great favour.

4 I prayed for their uplifting and not their downfall.

5 I cried in my heart with them as they cried and I had pity and sympathy for them even when their woes were simple.

6 Yeah, I prayed not for their hurt because I considered my iniquities.

7 I prayed not against them for the sake of not kindling hot coals over their heads.

8 Yea, these things have me down sincerely

9 Because of the mercy of my heart.

10 I truly prayed for their transgressions because I upheld the request to be forgiven by being forgiving.

11 This is the true sincerity of my soul and the Great Divine is my witness.

12 Because of the purity of my heart and the cleanliness of mind, I accepted dangerous blows from them that hate me without cause.

13 My goodness was repaid with evil for weakness.

14 Truly O Great Divine, Thou have searched my spirit and within, there was no guile to be found.

15 I punished myself greatly because of the burden of my transgressions.

16 They were continually before me and the weight of it overwhelmed me subconsciously.

17 Yea, shall I suffer mentally no more.

18 My heart has always invoked good things whenever it came towards Thee O Great Divine.

19 Truly the spirit is willing but the flesh is weak.

20 Now that my flesh is strengthened because of Thy generous mercies and sweet forgiveness, my spirit is waxed stronger.

21 Deliver me from all those who persecute my soul.

22 Their tongues stick out sharper than swords in which their mouths have become venomous and deadly.

23 Let their words of evil be their downfall just as Pharaoh had brought upon himself, his own seed and people.

24 They seek to destroy the son of the Most High Divine.

25 Therefore their children shall perish.

26 I prayed for their salvation because I never wished trouble upon them and in secret they plotted and stirred against my soul.

27 Therefore, in secret and at unawares shall they be brought to nought.

28 They build massive houses that are fortified strong and feel invincible within.

29 The Great Divine caused the Earth to shake terribly and moved its foundations.

30 Then a great tempest blew upon the face of the Earth and devoured them whole and greedily as a hungry lion.

31 Because of the truths of my heart and the contriteness of my spirit, the Most High Divine saved my life.

32 Thou had commanded that no sword shall pierce his flesh, neither bullets from guns nor shall any stones be cast make direct contact.

33 Not even a dog shall seek to bite thee for the Most High Divine had arise unto the preservation of my soul.

34 I daily commune with the Most High upon request because Thou had chosen me with Thine own hands.

35 Therefore, greatly shall I not be moved.

36 Mine enemies are no more, their tongues rot within their mouths and they have become abominable unto all.

37 Their memories are evanescent and their footsteps are erased from existence.

38 All because of the mercies of my soul and the sincere forgiveness of my heart it shall and will come to pass.

39 The Great Divine had known my name and sworn that Thou shall always hear the words of my mouth.

40 Whenever I call upon Thee, Thou shall hear and attend to the requests of my lips with suddenness and swiftness.

41 Men shall tremble at my presence because Thou had ordained me as a vessel to display Thy many powerful wonders.

42 I shall be satisfied with a long life. Blessed be the Mighty Most High Supreme Divine Being of antiquity. Amen.

PSALM 22

O merciful One, the Great Sovereignty that sits upon a most divine throne.

2 All times are surely in Thy Hands; Thou have a firm grip,

3 My times are surely within Thy Divine clutches.

4 Let me not be reproved amongst my people; let not the kin of my house forsake me.

5 Let me not be reproved amongst my neighbours; let not my friends become deceitful against me.

6 Give me great favour wherever I may go because of the uprightness and integrity of my heart.

7 Let me not be ashamed; let they be reproved amongst the face of men that try to slander my integrity.

8 Be swift unto my rescue from the tongues of men and all those who set themselves against me.

9 My times are in Thy Hands, therefore; Thou shall move faster than the speed of light to my aid.

10 Yea, Thou shall move swifter than that which moves faster than the speed of light

and even swifter than that to my distresses.

11 When Thou stand, all my enemies are turned around; rise O Great Divine and plead my cause.

12 Thou have pulled me out quickly before the gates of death were shut tight.

13 Therefore, I know the Most High Divine is for me so I am confident that the Most High Supreme shall preserve and keep me above all troubles.

PSALM 23

When my heart failed and I felt like all my hope was lost, I lifted my head unto Thee.

2 Where I am weak be my strength and where I am falling prop me on every side.

3 Where I am sick, give unto me the strength of thy youth.

4 Where there are plagues, give me deliverance and clear passage.

5 Where there is sorrow, give unto me great joy.

6 Where I am poor, make me rich and where I am hurt give me healing.

7 Where I am tired, give me rest and where I have failed, give me success.

8 Where there is famine, provide my feast and where there is drought; let my water well always be full.

9 Where there is evil, let me enjoy the sweet nectar of goodness.

10 Where there is imminent danger, let my protection be fortified.

11 Where there is the mist of death, let me be encased within the impenetrable shroud of Life.

12 The Great Divine said unto me is this all that thou desire of me?

13 Thou art my child in whom I am well pleased. The very sight of thee is a joy unto me.

14 For many generations I have awaited thee.

15 You asked of me for my knowledge, wisdom and overstanding over Life itself. You beseeched me for the true riches of Life.

16 You strive for love, peace and unity. You are truly forgiving for I have tested you personally.

17 You are a lover of thy neighbour, a help to the helpless even when you were also helplessly struggling.

18 Thou art my son in whom I am well pleased.

19 Therefore, greatly shall I bless thee and my goodness shall continuously be before thee.

20 I shall give unto thee unimaginable blessings and cause you to be higher than thy fellows. I shall greatly expand thy territories and heritage forevermore. Your seed too shall inherit the Earth.

21 This the Most High Divine had sworn to

uphold and shall never turn from it. I have become a pleasure in Thy sight, even Thy right eye. Selah.

PSALM 24

The love of the Great I AM is as potent as the intoxication of this illusion of human life.

2 When I am troubled by the woes of the flesh, the love of the Most High Divine has always been the reality of all things.

3 When my father had died and abandoned my kin and me in the flesh, the love of the Great Divine was forever abundant.

4 Yea, when I cried heavily, Thou had been my strong tower and a Father to the fatherless.

5 Thou had sent Thy love in various forms in which my eyes alone were opened up unto.

6 Truly at first, no one understands the plans of the Most High Divine.

7 All things are good, yea; all things are truly good indeed.

8 In the beginning, after Thou had ordained the works of Thy hands, Thou beheld it and said it is good.

9 Everything that has ever happened to me both the good and the bad, all were good.

10 Thou had blessed me with dreams of comfort; Thou had a

new prophet Samuel unto me. Yeah, I gained good fortune and the wording of my future.

11 Yea, the children did see my secret works and spoke to me unknowingly of it because of Thy love and goodness.

12 Thou had aligned my life in the same manner Thou had aligned the celestial order unto complete perfection.

13 Therefore, I shall not worry. My forgiveness came with an easy flow of a river that was at peace.

14 All things are good, there was never yet anything wrong that happened to me, yea; neither have I done any wrong in Thy sight.

15 My transgressions are blotted out from me; I am purged and made pure as liquid light.

16 My father had given up the ghost so that I could flourish; he helped unleash that hidden power within me.

17 The blessed Universal Saviour Divine had assured him of my greatness to be accomplished.

18 Today my soul rejoices because of the greatness the Most High Divine had laid up for my soul. Selah.

PSALM 25

How great is the Holy One that is above and beyond all things? Unimaginable!

2 Surely I shall put my trust in Thee O Most Mighty Divine Supreme.

3 When my faith was greatly tested, indeed I did reach at the precipice of my resolve.

4 Every time I reached my breaking point, thy mercies endured and persevered forevermore.

5 When the battle has become too stiff, Thou had relieved my soul and my worries.

6 Thou had shut up all my enemies alive within their tombs.

7 Not even their screams could be heard.

8 Thou had sealed them deep within a thick mountain and made them to be never seen or heard from again.

9 Thou had place betwixt them and me a great big desert; they all fainted and fell less than halfway across.

10 Thou had destroyed all their ships that they cannot meet me upon the other side of the ocean shores.

11 Yea, they had boats but the storms formed

and tossed them easily like rafts without sails.

12 They were left stranded and adrift and at the mercy of the mother ocean.

13 Yet still the seas obeyed the Great Divine and formed her whirlpool and spared none.

14 The Great Divine saw the error of their ways and saw that they indeed err in their hearts purposely without remorse and continuously with delight.

15 The words of their mouths are feigned, they flatter the Great Divine for mockery but deep within their souls, they abhor both righteousness and the righteous.

16 They continuously strive against the humble and those who are quiet in the land.

17 A great tempest and tornado shall arise to descend and ravish their tents and destroy their foods.

18 Famine and pestilence shall take them; they shall be caught within their own devices.

19 Their hands are marred and bloody with the hurt of the innocent, therefore; they shall be rewarded with the sword.

20 The Most High Divine had taken away the Holy Ghost from

them and they knew it not.

21 Thou had commissioned my anointing as the new king while the king that ruled was still in vigour and strength.

22 Yea, Thou had ordained such as Thou had commanded the prophet Samuel to anoint David king while Saul yet still ruled.

23 They transgressed against the Most High Supreme and purposed such in their hearts causing the Great Examiner to remove Thy Holy Covering.

24 They had invited the very ones who would eventually overthrow and replace them within their tents.

25 Never have I been a pest or a plague unto them but they strived to suppress my life.

26 The Saviour Divine had removed Thy Veil and they did entreat with their demise blindly.

27 Soon they are no more like Saul because they hated the Most High Divine from their hearts and in all that they do.

28 They have welcomed their destruction and have given them wine and provided merriment.

29 Their destruction has become inevitable and has been made to be perpetual.

30 My faith has been renewed because the Most High Divine is the very foundation in which I walk. Therefore I shall not stumble in the presence of man.

PSALM 26

O Great Supreme Being, the Great I AM THAT I AM.

2 Polarity has no hold upon Thee O Absolute Divine.

3 Because of Thee, polarity in its entirety exists.

4 I am confident in Thy strength and I'm sure of Thy honour.

5 Yea, shall I lift my eyes from whence cometh mine help.

6 Because of Thee, I have come to accept myself;

7 I am comfortable knowing that all things are good.

8 Therefore, I know I have been thoroughly purged.

9 My impurities are completely cleansed and burn away from me through the tests of fire.

10 My past only intended my future.

11 My mistakes were only intended for my perfection.

12 My errors and wrongs were only intended for my correction.

13 Yea, because of thy so-called sins was I made holy.

14 Yea, because of my adversities, I beheld the truth.

15 Not just any truth but the entire truth indeed did I behold.

16 I gained the secrets of the Universe and came to know the Origins of all things.

17 Yea, I have come to know the very Origins of the Most High Supreme Divine Being.

18 With Thee, what goes up surely doesn't have to come back down.

19 And what goes around does not have to come back around.

20 I am thoroughly cleansed because I am a part of the Grand Master's Design. I was engineered to be aligned with the Great Divine of Supreme Consciousness.

21 Therefore, shall I rejoice in Thy strength eternally O Great All in All Most High Divine.

PSALM 27

Humbly I place myself before Thee O Holy Divine Presence.

2 Humbly I seek the knowledge of Your wisdom from Thy inward parts O Most High Supreme.

3 Grant unto me Your answers in the visions of truth at night.

4 Yea, give it unto me at the times when my body goes to sleep but when my spirit awakes.

5 Grant me the answers which I seek from the friends upon which I can truly lean.

6 Yea, let them be used as an instrument both directly and indirectly according to Thy will because Thou had appointed them unto me.

7 Provide the responses I seek from the babes and suckling because in them Thou have truly ordained strength.

8 Yea, they are closer to the source of creation and are filled with the goodness of the ineffable Most High Supreme Divine Being.

9 Bless me with the answers through nature; as the wind blows and as the trees sway give it Thou unto me.

10 O merciful and Great Holy Divine, grant me all the answers I seek in all forms and fashion. Give me the vision to differentiate.

11 Yea, shall I behold it because I begat the eye to see beyond.

12 I possess the internal ear to hear that which cannot be heard.

13 I was blessed with that spiritual sense of touch to feel the slightest change in frequencies.

14 Yea, many secrets shall be opened up unto me because of Thy Divine will.

15 Yea, I shall escape from judgment unto salvation because of Thy Holy Name's sake.

16 Humbly I place myself before Thee always O Holy Divine Presence. Preserve the king's life and his years as many generations.

PSALM 28

The most ungrateful act is to not be contented when we are given something of true value.

2 Our eyes can see things bigger or smaller than it appears.

3 It all depends upon the perspective of our thoughts and how we choose to view such.

4 Limited in mind is the man who genuinely believes he can never lift an entire tree.

5 It may not be so as with the actual tree itself being fully grown.

6 But upon carrying a seed, one never knew the enormity of the tree that exists within.

7 Sometimes our blessings come in the package of a little mustard seed.

8 But with nurture and care it is yielded into a colossal behemoth of uncountable blessings.

9 It is good to be grateful unto the Most High Supreme always.

10 Honour the Absolute Divine with contentedness and watch everything you have been multiplied and replenished beyond measure.

PSALM 29

All of our days have proven to be filled with vanity.

2 Vain are the works of the hands that practice necromancy.

3 Nonsensical are the works of sorcery and witchcraft to hurt the innocent.

4 The Earth is a free place and now many have become trapped by debt.

5 Tell me what is all the fussing and fighting about?

6 O merciful Divine, all our days are filled with vanity.

7 In my dismay at the world, I questioned how this existence is even possible.

8 A man shall work all his days and heap up vanities from which his soul shall flee.

9 His soul does escape the clutches of his fingers and yet still his life is based solely upon the heaping treasures.

10 Superficiality has caused many to seek after vanity superfluously.

11 Yeah, they seek after death more than living life itself.

12 Death is easy but spiritual damnation is the worst thing unto those that are truly

uneven in all their essence.

13 All war and strife are vain.

14 Ego is the greatest devil that can dwell in anyone once uncontrollable.

15 O Great Divine, Your people have become so trapped that they kill the ones that bring about freedom.

16 They do oppress the awakeners of spirit.

17 They oppress and downtrodden the ones delivering tormented souls.

18 And yet still they accept the oppressors with open arms.

19 Yea the wicked shall perish because of frivolity.

20 All our days are vanity.

21 But fulfilling are our walks in righteousness and being balanced with a nature of divinity that leads to eternal bliss.

22 To exist eternally is the greatest riches because when all wickedness fades, yet still I AM.

PSALM 30

Yea, the shackles have been lifted and been broken.

2 The captives have been freed.

3 When my soul was in trouble, I still trusted in the Most High Supreme.

4 The power of Thy strength was manifested before me.

5 Thou silenced those in high places because of the sake of the low.

6 Thou had shut up the mouth of the mighty man because of the tongue of the meek.

7 Thou had banded tightly together the powers of principalities and spiritual wickedness in high places that were against me.

8 Surely the Most High Divine had delivered my soul to be free as the fishes of the seas and as the birds that soar high. Selah.

PSALM 31

The oppression of my soul is blown out as a candle.

2 Their wind is still and Life does not blow in abundance upon their lot.

3 Yet my strength prevailed against their storms and tempests.

4 My feet walked perfectly through their landmines.

5 Where they dug their pits, I became light as a feather as I crossed it.

6 Where they planted firmly their mischievous devices, I became heavy to trample it.

7 I have become a wonder unto many because of the mystics of the Most High Supreme Holy Divine Being.

8 I have now become a symbol of fear upon my foes but hope and strength to the weak.

9 Their tongues tremble at the sound of my name.

10 Their hearts fail at the very sight of me.

11 They bow their heads within my presence just as the tares beneath a huge tree.

12 My roots have been planted firmly in solid yet fertile ground.

13 Because of the Great Supreme; even the Absolute Divine have I been made strong to last longer than the will of all mine adversaries.

PSALM 32

Blessed be the name of the Most High Divine Supreme.

2 The Great Divine is the protector of my life.

3 The Great Divine is the Director of my steps intuitively.

4 The Great Divine is the provider of my needs.

5 The Great Divine of Hosts is the answer before and for all my supplications.

6 The Great Divine had already ordained my successes.

7 The Great Divine had crowned my head with royalty.

8 It is great to give thanks unto the Most High Supreme Divine.

9 Thou have truly been great unto me.

10 All I had to do was look at all the things I was blinded unto.

11 The lands were formed, the seas were established and the fruits of the Earth were made just for me.

12 Yea, the clouds and the stars; the sun and moon all work in correlation to the benefit of my being.

13 Yea, the Spirit of the Most High

Supreme dwells within the temples of flesh in which Life was given.

14 Yea, I became a living soul because of Thee O Most High Divine.

15 Thou surely would never save me from mine enemies to only allow for my recapture to once again become ensnared by them.

16 When Thou catch my feet from slipping, it is not that I should fall afterwards.

17 When I see that Thou have delivered my soul from trouble, then I was truly made to know Thy power.

18 For this, I know the Most High Divine is for me. Thou continue to reveal what was blatantly hidden from me.

19 Therefore, I know my deliverance is continuously forthcoming.

20 My breakthroughs are guaranteed because of the Most Mighty Divine.

21 Blessed be the name of the Almighty Most High Supreme.

PSALM 33

I AM THAT I AM: The Most Magnificent, the Absolute Nothing that begat Everything.

2 I AM THAT I AM: The Most Unexplainable Phenomenon that existed eternally before the inception of all Beginnings.

3 I AM THAT I AM. unto Thee, I do call. Your holy language is beyond the comprehension of my simple speech.

4 How can I know and yet still not know at the same time?

5 It is a feeling that can be felt but yet still cannot be explained by the physical tongue.

6 Thou Art a Majestic Experience. To gain common insight is to experience Thee O Almighty Supreme; individually.

7 Thou have spoken in silence and I have heard it, therefore; shall my soul be at peace and my spirit at rest.

8 I AM THAT I AM said the Mysteriously Universal Supreme Divine Being that many have been in search of.

9 I AM the Most Precious Divine over all other divinities.

10 I AM Salvation.

11 I AM the All in All.

12 I AM Truth.

13 I AM the Natural Mystic.

14 I AM Protection. I AM Deliverance. I AM the Uplifting Fulfillment.

15 I AM Tenderness. I AM Help. I AM Divine Favour.

16 I AM Perfect. I AM Fullness. I AM Calm.

17 I AM Infinite; I AM Creation. I AM All Things.

18 I AM Magical. I AM Reality. I AM Almighty.

19 I AM Everywhere and Anywhere.

20 I AM THAT I AM. There is no place I cannot be found.

21 My Presence is known within the heavens and in the hell of things I AM present at all times.

22 Be still and know that I AM THAT I AM unto thee O blessed child. I AM Peace and Justice. I AM Liberty.

23 All I require of you to do is just believe in yourself that all things are possible.

24 Have a little faith and believe in yourself and be still in mind.

25 Know that I have never failed once because I AM THAT I AM.

PSALM 34

O how foolish is the man that put his trust in warfare and weaponry?

2 O how foolish are they that put their trust unto blood sacrifice and abominable feasts?

3 O how foolish are they that solely put their trust in soothsayers and works of obeah?

4 O how foolish are they that put their trust in vanity to save their souls?

5 As for me, many days have my life been in regret and resentment.

6 Many days were I out of breath because of my heavy sighing.

7 My countenance did drop and my flesh shrunk because of my regretful mourning.

8 Yea, I have indiscriminately judged myself harsher than that of the Great Most High Divine.

9 The Almighty Supreme Divine had become disturbed by the punishment that I had bestowed upon myself.

10 How foolish of me to have forgotten the glory of the Holy One who had ordained my walk aeons before my flesh even existed?

11 The Most Mighty Supreme had rescued me from myself.

12 Yeah, I have become my own worst enemy. I was defeated within my abode.

13 Therefore, I lay myself before my enemies to be conquered.

14 How foolish was I to strip away my strength to be rendered spiritually impotent?

15 The only help I can beg of my enemies is to take my life.

16 I saw the strength of man and was blinded to the strength of the Most High Divine from within.

17 Yea though my eyes see I was yet still devoid of vision.

18 How can I trust more in the powers of men because of the fear of their strength?

19 Foolish it was of me but foolish I am no more because of Thy Holy Grace.

20 No man can be stronger than Thee O Most Mighty Divine.

21 All men still need the air that cometh from Thy Nostrils O Mighty Divine.

22 They all need the waters of Life that flow from Thy Holy Eyes.

23 They still need the fruits that come from

the loins of the Almighty Supreme.

24 We fear not what we cannot see, whereby many do choose to pledge their allegiance and loyalty to that which is solely visible and tangible.

25 Yeah, many trust in man, others in weapons, some in money and others in power.

26 As for me I shall trust in Thee O Most Holy Divine.

27 At any time asteroids can rain down upon Earth and men fear not.

28 There are so many colossal dangers out in the space of heaven and men fear not.

29 I shall not worry at all about man and the horrors of the flesh.

30 The same way huge planets such as Jupiter have been a shield from Earth's oblivion Thou shall be unto me.

31 What shall I fear; my past, my present or my future?

32 Thou have saved the Earth from uncountable annihilation and this I know to be true. Therefore, whom shall I fear?

33 Therefore, how foolish it was of me to not behold Thy perfectly natural wonders?

34 My problems are nothing unto Thee and

Thou have vowed to save me and answer me whenever I call; for Thou is familiar with all the tones of my voice. Blessed be the Saviour Divine Being of my soul.

PSALM 35

Blessed be the Universal Most High Divine; the Great Architect beyond this grand design.

2 How elaborate are the works of thy fingers that are so complex with detailed analysis but yet still simplistic unto common understanding?

3 Yeah, I have been integrated into this grand design that is orchestrated by Your Hands O Most Divine Source.

4 Sometimes it is confusing to understand my role especially when I am in fear of the flesh.

5 Especially when I worry about the past; especially when I worry about the future, whereby; my present life is turned into an unbearable burden to live.

6 Comfort me in all my discomforts and save my thoughts from pessimism.

7 Bless me with the joy and strength of a perfect but realistic optimism.

8 Make me to know of my importance unto Thee. O Most High Divine, show forth Thy wonders unto me.

9 Yea, Thou have given me confidence that is now unwavering.

10 I felt the strength of Thy bliss and when I worry I longed for it because I did remember such a feeling.

11 When I rocked to and fro within my soul, I walked forward and then turned back but the beauty of Thy Majesty I recollected.

12 Give me the strength to make that leap of faith;

13 Let me stand firm in Thy strength in that I shall not one bit be moved.

14 Let me stand strong as a great pillar, even a mountain so when turbulence passes by, I shall not be moved and it shall be broken down into a gentle wind.

15 Yea, I shall never give up because my help cometh from a Source Most Mighty and Supremely Divine.

PSALM 36

O Holy Divine, the storms have ceased.

2 The tempests have been blown away.

3 The roaring waters have been calmed;

4 And the rough waves have been broken down unto tranquillity.

5 Yea, it was made safe for my feet to tread upon the shores of the seas.

6 The seas were filled with fish that my breadbasket never ran empty.

7 The oceans have washed up its sunken treasures unto me.

8 I am made to be exceedingly glad and my entire life was allowed to turn into a constant celebration for all the sadness my tormented soul had to endure.

9 In my times of trouble I had chosen to put my trust in the Most High Divine.

10 When I gave up all hope, my faith even though miniscule, I cast it upon the stairs of the Almighty Divine.

11 It budded instantaneously and grew in at once.

12 The soil of the Great I AM is beyond magical and needs no time.

13 My heart was overwhelmed with the blessings of Thy Holy Countenance.

14 My blessings have become so much that I know not what shall I do with it all. I have now become an overnight blessing unto many I've encountered.

15 My oil pan was filled until it overflowed exceedingly as a waterfall; it poured upon me and gathered itself as the ocean.

16 When the Supreme Divine of Hosts began to bless me, I felt the sudden urge to hide myself.

17 I wondered what I had done to deserve such treatment of royalty. But I remembered how much I had lost and sacrificed while trying to discover my divine purpose.

18 But even though I had lost faith, I never stopped practising goodness.

19 My soul shall always be in peace, my soul shall perpetually be at peace, yea; my soul shall forever dwell in peace eternally.

PSALM 37

Yea, I have acknowledged my shortcomings.

2 For my atonement, good tidings I rendered unto the ones in which I have transgressed.

3 I easily forgive those who have transgressed against me at all times.

4 Yea, I have borne such a burden upon my head.

5 Yea, I suffered the blows of those that hate me and yet still I nursed their wounds.

6 When they saw me, they sent for poison to heal my sores.

7 I entreated them with favour and gave them water and savoury drink when they thirsted.

8 But as for me, they masked vinegar and poured it into my drink to torture my soul.

9 When they were tired, I gave them to rest on my bed.

10 But yeah, I was cast upon the cold floor to sleep as a dog.

11 I troubled my soul because of them for my righteousness's sake.

12 I seek their favour at the sake of my soul in which I jeopardised my wellbeing.

13 For this have I gained great divine favour. Yea, great divine favour because the merciful I AM saw that my intent was genuine.

14 Yeah, my worrying and atonement were more than I could bear.

15 My blessed Saviour Divine had pardoned me as I severely punished myself mentally.

16 But now I have become their end.

17 They repaid my kindness with maliciousness and advantage and in their hearts they have no forgiveness.

18 I changed because of my circumstances but they remained stagnant.

19 The Most High Divine shall give unto them a hundred folds of the torment they brought.

20 It shall be too heavy for them because they have no love in their hearts.

21 They shall be a reproach amongst men and they shall pray to be swallowed alive.

22 Be careful of those whom you throw stones and cast judgment upon.

23 I am a beloved creation of the Universal Most High

Supreme Divine Being who shall continuously avenge me of my enemies and those who rise against me in judgment.

24 Not a finger shall I raise; neither shall I utter a word because I shall be comfortably hidden amidst the divine shadows of the Great Divine.

PSALM 38

In the same way the Merciful Divine prevents us with Its Universal goodness; it is in the same we can be chastened by it.

2 When I pray earnestly for my enemies and those that hate me it is because of such they shall be reduced to naught.

3 When I pray sincerely for those who persecute and revile me, it is that I become their end.

4 When I pray reverently for those who stick their tongues out against me in judgment that their words penetrate my soul as a dagger;

5 It is that they shall be shut up forevermore and be ashamed.

6 I pity all those who choose to stand against many and raise their tongues in judgment because they know not what lies ahead for them.

7 Daily have I received confirmation of the salvation of the Great and Merciful Divine.

8 It is that when men puff up at me, with immediate haste shall the Great Divine puff up to strike them down.

9 Test not the resolve of the Holy Divine One because my help is swifter than that which is known as the fastest unto the knowledge of mortals.

10 A blow from the Almighty Saviour Divine is worse than any plague.

11 Lest the Most High Supreme take pity upon them, they shall suffer a great suffering.

12 Lest the Most High grant them pardon, they are withered up and consumed.

13 If the Most High Supreme withholds Thy loving kindnesses from them, surely they are no more in remembrance.

14 Yea, do I pray for mine enemies and those that hate me mercilessly.

15 They stop not because they have been caught up in the worry of their own devices.

16 The Great Sovereign Divine is my refuge and as I pray for my foes, my hands are washed and cleaned.

17 Their downfall I am never guilty of because I do pray for the uplifting of their souls but they turn not from their malevolent ways. Selah.

PSALM 39

It is good for me to extend gratitude to the Universe daily;

2 In that my steps shall be guided thoroughly.

3 I shall tread in peace and safety and the abundance of protection.

4 My soul shall be at peace and I shall never suffer corruption because in my tongue there is exceeding gratitude.

5 Early every morning do I extend praises unto the Most High Supreme, even subconsciously.

6 Every night I shall fill my soul by offering the praises of thanksgiving.

7 In the night time I shall offer up my prayers because I shall not be removed in my glory.

8 As I lay down to sleep; the enemy believes me to be vulnerable in that they wish to launch their secret attacks.

9 They wish to catch me with the element of surprise.

10 But yeah, it would have been that easy if the Supreme Divine had not been for me.

11 In my sleep they tried to take my life through spite works

but the Great Watcher that watches over me never needs sleep.

12 My spirit was made strong in that the perpetrators were revealed unto me.

13 I was given the strength to conquer them spiritually, yea; I shall not lay a finger upon them.

14 Yet they perish at the will of my purity.

15 Nasty a fight they waged against me secretly but their plots are revealed and they became sick unto death by the stench of their filth.

16 Their ways are caught up to them; they turn not in that they would have surely escaped their judgments.

17 The Most High Divine had accepted them and had been far too lenient with them.

18 Through intended oppression, they made the child of the Holy One stronger but each time I have proven myself further.

19 My sighing went up and angry it made the Supreme Divine.

20 As they move in secret at my soul, the Most High Divine had revealed Thyself boldly.

21 From the secret place, Thou have appeared unto them boldly and in a form most terrible.

22 In their secret places, the Most High Divine strikes them from the heart.

23 In their safe places, the Almighty Supreme brought great danger upon them.

24 Thou have risen to plead my cause and now they shall bother me no more.

25 The holy child have they fought against for far too long; the Great Divine said no more.

26 Thou have declared that enough is enough.

27 Suddenly they are no more, they are cut off forever and my soul is at peace.

28 My soul is at great peace and my restless nights turned into harmony.

29 My mourning has been turned into dancing because I acknowledge and talk with the Great Divine daily.

30 In every little way possible, I choose to give thanks as often as I can.

PSALM 40

The flesh is of a finite principle that is yet still infinite.

2 Crack open the shallowness of the carnal mind and you shall see clearly.

3 Within the man, he contains all the seeds to conceive an infinite amount of offspring.

4 Within the woman, she contains all the eggs to be impregnated for an eternity.

5 Yet still within each apparatus responsible for natural procreation, infinity exists within itself and within that which is within perpetually.

6 Therefore, is it wise to think finite when you are already in possession of infinity?

7 The Great Divine Source is in existence in a Holy Place that is eternally unknown.

8 Yet still, this unknown place where this Great Divine Source abides can be found within the soul operating in Its microcosm process.

9 Self-healing is a must once you believe in SELF without a doubt.

10 Limit not thyself ye great men of the spirit.

11 You are nature's unlimited

programming that was designed to be limitless by nature both finite and infinite. Selah.

PSALM 41

O blessed Almighty Saviour Divine,

2 Heed my call and hear my plea;

3 Thou have revealed my strong enemies and for this, I am grateful indeed.

4 Yea, direct my steps in that I may seek wise counsel from Thee intuitively at all times.

5 Thou have taught me to be immaculate in my actions and words in that I bring about no further burdens upon my head.

6 But O Great Divine Supreme, I beseech Thee to protect me from those closest to me.

7 Many a time have I borne witness to the fall of great men.

8 They did indeed fall because of the betrayal of those who break bread with them.

9 They did open up their homes to them and they were full of deceit.

10 O Great Supreme Divine, I beseech Thee to catch them within their own snares.

11 If there be a chance that their minds can be deterred, ensure it is so but if their intent be fixed, be swift to my rescue Superior Divine.

12 Let not the love of my heart be the destruction of me.

13 Let not the love of my heart blind me from the reality of the heinous nature behind those smiles of silent maniacal deception.

14 Spare my life from all manner of evil, rancour and deadly calumnies. Let not my heart be troubled.

15 Pass me over from glory unto glory. Grant me divine blessings after blessings abundantly as I live to be fat with age.

16 My soul shall forever jump for joy because the Most Magnificent Divine is for me always. Selah.

PSALM 42

Early on in my life, I began searching for my purpose.

2 I began my pursuit to understand who or what exactly is the Most High Divine.

3 I began to search every possible nook and corner of the Earth in my mind by devoting myself to research.

4 I tried to decode from the grass to the trees and from a stone to a mountain.

5 It was not fulfilling so I began to explore the depths of space as I explored my mind as a spiritual astronaut.

7 This wild goose chase to find the Grand Supreme was both amusing and revealing.

8 I searched everywhere possible, save for the place I left almost deserted.

9 The thing is many just regard our vessels to be just a body.

10 This cloak of flesh is the covering of a Most Divine Spark from the uncovered Source that is shrouded in divine darkness in the same manner our clothing keeps hidden in our most private areas.

11 I failed to learn about that which was already hidden to be found within my soul.

12 The more I began to learn about myself, the more I found myself.

13 And the more I found myself, the more I unfolded and decoded and profoundly discovered mystical realisations about the truly indescribable Essence of the Almighty Source Divine.

14 As I discovered this Holy Essence of my Being, I began to discover and unfold my purpose in full.

15 Now I am a natural wonder unto many but more so unto myself.

16 Blessed be the Universal Magnificent Most High Supreme Divine Being that is very much Omnipresent, Omnipotent and Omniscient within my soul.

PSALM 43

Be mindful that the anointing of the Absolute Divine brings treachery.

2 Even though Saul was the ruler and at first exalted David, he became envious and jealous of the little shepherd boy's accomplishments.

3 A king became jealous of a common lad in society.

4 Yea, it was the natural anointing upon his life that he was envied and abhorred for.

5 Yea I have been envied by one that sits in a high seat.

6 No promotion came by his hands to the modern shepherd boy who worked diligently for the leader of prominence.

7 Nothing but a dream I came with and a passion purified by the trials of fire.

8 From the prominent public figure I did seek assistance earnestly.

9 His words did come from flattering lips but his envy and jealousy were long before revealed unto me by the Most Mighty Divine.

10 The time has passed and it came to pass.

11 I was left with empty promises and

shallow words that were made to sound with a guarantee from feigned lips and assertiveness.

12 I was hurt indeed as I had to return home empty-handed with no means to supply my breadbasket.

13 From your own people, you can face the most fights and are never without foe.

14 I was made to endure even though I genuinely felt like giving up;

15 For my life have consistently been trials after trials.

16 I was seeking a small breakthrough for once and was met with sore disappointment after my tenure had ended.

17 I was tested and purified once again. My help cometh from the Most High Supreme in that no man can take credit for and from me. I was self-taught spiritually from the Great Divine within me.

18 I was promoted in more ways than one.

19 Just like David was anointed king before he inherited his kingdom, so too was I ordained.

20 Yea I shall never be dethroned by my own hands like Saul did to himself.

21 Yea, shall none that rise against me shall

be able to take my crown of glory.

22 The blessed Most High Supreme Divine is for me at all times and throughout all seasons.

23 I shall be fat with Thy goodness and the hidden treasures that Thou have laid up for the restitution of my soul.

24 Yea I shall be a most benevolent leader and a beloved example to and by countless millions.

25 My provinces shall be greatly multiplied;

26 And my borders extend beyond foreign territories.

27 The blessings of the Most Royal Divine have been bestowed upon me, therefore; I shall rejoice in Thy Glory. My life shall be saturated with age to rule and reign supreme until the very end. My seeds shall too inherit the Earth because Thy mercy endures forever.

PSALM 44

Love is the conduit the entire Universe expresses Itself.

2 Every great man is always in pursuit of an even greater woman to bring out the best in him.

3 Show me clearly the pathway O Universal Divine and grant unto me the one whom my heart desires.

4 Holy Matrimony had Thou O Holy One already established cosmologically in that Thou have never been lacking companionship.

5 Always in Holy Communion are both the cosmological Divine Feminine and Divine Masculine.

6 Now that Your child has departed from thy mother's bosom, prepare thy spouse to be clean and pure internally.

7 Ask and it shall be granted unto you when the time is right said the Great Divine.

8 Eternity; the waits seems to be unto the flesh that is mandated by time.

9 All this loneliness with no one to truly understand; and barely anyone to trust caused me to be withdrawn by my thoughts as an

introvert within myself.

10 Low self-esteem as I continuously searched the world within my comfort zone.

11 Look at Jacob and how he had to work an additional seven years, apart from his initial seven before he could finally marry the love of his life Rachel.

12 I too have been toiling away doing my divine duties awaiting my pay.

13 Satisfy my life with the completion of my better half O Supreme Divine.

14 Hallowed shall her steps be in which Thou have guided unto the doorsteps of my heart and likewise I unto hers.

15 Ask of me a wife and I shall grant unto thee a goddess O child; just be patient.

16 Let not your heart be troubled because I have already ordained unto thee perfect inheritance.

17 Everything has already been granted unto you long before you even made a single request physically.

18 All thy offspring shall be divine and a wondrous sight to behold.

19 Claim what you know to be rightfully yours and greater

things shall be added unto thee.

20 Offer up all thy sacrifices as a love offering unto the Universal Divine Supreme.

21 Covetous shall many be over her but her devotion shall be unto thee.

22 King I have already ordained thee, your queen I have already revealed unto thee both spiritually and physically.

23 Do well by each other's side and flourish beyond measure.

24 Understanding shall be the foundation of your holy union.

25 Blessed shall thy union be in Thy Sight O Universal Divine because it is the workings of Thy Holy Hands.

26 Energy never dies for it is the Love of the Universe that had banded us together to become an oasis to each other's desert. Our energies are forever entwined as we joined together as our Cosmic Divinities before us for an eternity. Asé.

PSALM 45

I feel pity for those who practice sorcery for the hurt of those innocent without cause.

2 They see not the severity in which they stun their growth both physically and spiritually.

3 How long shall the wicked reign and imagine vain things?

4 Paranoid they become because of the silent movements of the Universal Supreme Divine Being.

5 They keep watch of the slippery paths they set just to witness the footings of the righteous in heart slip and fall for good.

6 But when their expectations are met with disappointment, they ask how.

7 Bad-mind, negative and evil thoughts are the fuel for sorcery to work.

8 But purity and positivity of mind are the ultimate deflection of such.

9 The obeah workers do sink themselves deeper each time they put their hands to renew their spite works.

10 Their minds begin to play a terrible trick on them.

11 When the ones they attack show no symptoms, they begin to feel as if they are returning the favour.

12 They are unable to see that their subconscious mind has become their own worst enemy because they have betrayed themselves. It is now the Universal Principle at play.

13 Most even continue down the same path unto spiritual condemnation because they are unable to face themselves.

14 They plague their children and curse their entire generation.

15 But when the night of weeping has been endured by the righteous, their joy came to stay because their foes are rendered impotent perpetually.

16 Our help is from the Universal Most High Supreme that represents perfect balance.

PSALM 46

Uncertainty of the mind can very much lead to untimely occurrences.

2 Having a sound mind is indeed a great blessing to ask of the Supreme Divine.

3 Help guard my thoughts O Precious Divine.

4 Prevent me thoroughly with the mercies of Thy goodness.

5 No accidents shall befall me neither any untimely occurrences.

6 Let me be in sync with the Universal pulse and ultra instinct.

7 Prevent my steps from sudden demise and from dangers at times unaware.

8 Let no bones be broken within my vessel.

9 Cause me to never dash my feet against any stone.

10 Universally divine protections are the holy garments of Your children.

PSALM 47

A seed must first be planted for it to grow.

2 Death is a nonexistent claim made by mere mortal instruments of flesh.

3 Indeed the outer husk of the seed withers away in that it is inevitable to take new form. But once planted, the eye within shall resurrect.

4 In Life there are many deaths encountered but all lead to the same thing; transition.

5 Indeed the eye of the seed is very tender at first but strong enough to rise out from the ground on its own, for the Earth is an ever-living being.

6 There is nothing wrong in mourning a loved one who has passed on from time into the ethereal realm.

7 It is imperative that you stop associating the term Rest in Peace to your ancestors who came before you.

8 Energy needs not rest.

9 The body initially began as a seed that germinated within the fertile soil of the womb, in days of three.

10 During its lifetime, it replicates itself through the

reproductive parts within both the man and woman.

11 Upon its final transitioning stage which is generally regarded as death, it goes back to its initial stages as a seed to be replanted.

12 This time around, it is the "I" that shall rise unto a new transformation within the esoteric plain. Hence, it is imperative to seek the balance of SELF.

13 Grant your ancestors your energy of love to help them further Rise In Power instead.

14 The happy planter will always add unto the vitality of his planted crops at all times; the way it bears naturally will be evident enough.

15 This way it is more beneficial unto him and many others.

16 Stop suppressing your ancestral linkages because the barrier your grief creates will not permit them to help you spiritually.

17 They are always willing to assist and support you at all times but all you need to do is ask and believe. Love is the plug, therefore; celebrate Life at all times.

PSALM 48

O Mighty Most High Divine;

2 How great a battlefield is the mind?

3 It is the ultimate play park in which thoughts interact with each other.

4 Many a time they are in great conflict.

5 Many times there are manipulations of thoughts by rogue elements unseen to the natural eyes.

6 Anoint my head with Thy Spiritual Ointment and cover the uppermost chamber of my dwelling.

7 Conflicting thoughts have caused many to take their own lives.

8 They entertain foreign forces unbeknown to them.

9 They do torment those who have lowered their vibrations as they cluster their mind with confusion and a furry of thoughts.

10 The man who is truly conscious in mind would not allow such manipulation in that he would embody such heinous actions physically towards another by encouraging the mental destruction of others.

11 Many foreign forces are envious of most dwellers in the flesh because many have divinity and they seek to possess any who allows them to do such subconsciously.

12 It is a blessing to be aligned with the Most Holy Divine in that one is continuously trained to increase one's overall vibration to surf above all on the ever-growing Universal Wave.

PSALM 49

The masses of Thy people have fallen victim to a great spell and curse Saviour Divine.

2 A spell that is of mental proportions.

3 They see but are yet still blinded.

4 They hear and are yet still deafened.

5 The yoke is strongly attached to their necks and shackled to their brains.

6 Yet still they do not seek to become in tune with themselves to be fattened properly with truthful knowledge to break free mentally.

7 They prefer to drink from the cup of drought and eat from the plate of famine.

8 They accept a barren wasteland and willfully abnegate their once beloved and flourishing homelands.

9 They discard enlightenment to bask in the blackness of ignorance through a lack of knowledge of light.

10 Rip the veils from their eyes O Mighty Supreme Divine lest they sleep eternally spiritually.

11 Oppression has become the new norm and imprisonment is

the new form of freedom.

12 Negativity has become the order of the day with little positivity in sight.

13 Arise O Mighty Universal Divine, the Great Shift is already upon us for Thy Will shall be done. Only those awakened shall rejoice. Amen and Amen.

PSALM 50

One night my intuition guided me to carry out a simple mission.

2 I whispered into my youngest brother's ear gently, calling out his name as he slept.

3 I repeated such only a few times ensuring that I didn't wake him.

4 Early the next morning I had asked him if he had dreamt anything.

5 "Yes, he responded. I kept hearing you calling me and I was answering and looking for you and couldn't find you."

6 He said that he almost began to cry.

7 Guard us O Saviour Divine from external forces who try to manipulate our dreams to trigger off a negative reality in our awakening life.

8 Protect our spirits from wandering off too far as we sleep.

9 O Holy Divine, keep watch over my soul so that I may not be cut short untimely within my sleep.

10 How great is the Great Divine indeed? Thou have shown me many great things that are simply overlooked.

PSALM 51

The might of the Most High Supreme have caused my enemies to be at peace with me.

2 They have become docile at the might of the Absolute Divine.

3 They have become canaries to sing of my praises.

4 I rejoiced not in the downfall of man but at the blessings extended unto me by the Most Holy Divine.

5 My only wish is that we all can live in peace but envy and jealousy are thorns in the eyes and hearts of men.

6 The weeds are exterminated from within my growing space.

7 I am now able to extend my branches and my roots are made stronger than before.

8 I have become fruitful beyond measure.

9 My treasure chambers are now widened and filled with precious gems and rare metals and earthly wealth because of the Great Divine I have treasured above all things.

10 My eyes are now made to keep steadfast but I am comforted in the fact

that none can ever stop the man of spirit.

11 My wings are now able to soar without hindrance. Amen.

PSALM 52

The shackles of fear have been detached from my soul.

2 It was an anchor to my divine purpose.

3 It was a millstone upon my neck.

4 I suffered greatly because of it, yea; it was my mortal nemesis spiritually.

5 My destiny was calling me and I was too scared to answer it.

6 I struggled greatly as I battled against the enemy of my thoughts.

7 I blanked my mind with the little courage I found and followed through as I called upon the Divine Supreme.

8 From time to time I had to be reminded about myself.

9 Many times we are too caught up within the matrix of human complexities.

10 We lose our identities and accept peasantry over royalty.

11 It takes great courage and strength to remind yourself constantly to always remember who you truly are at all times.

12 In this illusion of multiplicities, many succumb to fear and can easily be swept away by the many

ever-present distractions.

13 But if it had not been for the reality of the Divine Source, my soul too would have been lost.

14 Yea, I have befriended my fears and now I am master over my destiny. Selah.

www.ingramcontent.com/pod-product-compliance
Lightning Source LLC
LaVergne TN
LVHW021355080426
835508LV00020B/2289